W9-CJG-920

A BEACON BIOGRAPHY

Carson Wentz

Pete DiPrimio

PURPLE TOAD
PUBLISHING

PURPLE TOAD
PUBLISHING

Copyright © 2019 by Purple Toad Publishing, Inc. Updated and reprinted, 2019. All rights reserved. No part of this book may be reproduced without written permission from the publisher. Printed and bound in the United States
of America.

Printing   1   2   3   4   5   6   7   8   9

A Beacon Biography

Angelina Jolie
Anthony Davis
Ben Simmons
Big Time Rush
Bill Nye
Cam Newton
Carly Rae Jepsen
Carson Wentz
Chadwick Boseman
Daisy Ridley
Drake
Ed Sheeran
Ellen DeGeneres
Elon Musk
Ezekiel Elliott
Gal Gadot
Harry Styles of One Direction
Jennifer Lawrence
Joel Embiid
John Boyega

Kevin Durant
Lorde
Malala
Maria von Trapp
Markus "Notch" Persson, Creator of Minecraft
Meghan Markle
Michelle Obama
Millie Bobby Brown
Misty Copeland
Mo'ne Davis
Muhammad Ali
Neil deGrasse Tyson
Oprah Winfrey
Peyton Manning
Robert Griffin III (RG3)
Stephen Colbert
Stephen Curry
Tom Holland
Zendaya

Library of Congress Cataloging-in-Publication Data
DiPrimio, Pete.
   Carson Wentz / Written by Pete DiPrimio.
      p. cm.
Includes bibliographic references, glossary, and index.
ISBN 9781624694622
1. Wentz, Carson. 1992- — Juvenile literature. 2. Football players — Juvenile literature. 3. North Dakota State University — Football — Juvenile literature 4. Philadelphia Eagles — NFL — Biography — Juvenile literature. I. Series: A Beacon Biography

GV939.W46A45 2019
Carson 796.332
[B]
Library of Congress Control Number: 2018945779

eBook ISBN: 9781624694639

ABOUT THE AUTHOR: Pete DiPrimio is an award-winning sports writer for the *Fort Wayne [Indiana] News-Sentinel*, a longtime freelance writer, and a member of the Indiana Sportswriters and Sports Broadcasters Hall of Fame. He has been an adjunct lecturer for the National Sports Journalism Center at IUPU-Indianapolis and for Indiana University's School of Journalism. He is the author of three nonfiction books pertaining to Indiana University athletics and more than 20 books for young readers. Pete is also a fitness instructor, plus a tennis, racquetball, biking, and weightlifting enthusiast.

PUBLISHER'S NOTE: This story has not been authorized or endorsed by Carson Wentz.

CONTENTS

When Carson Wentz came to Philadelphia, people had a lot of questions about him. He answered them with a record-setting rookie season to remember.

The Beginning

Why would Carson Wentz do it?

He was a potential superstar quarterback, a promising Philadelphia Eagles rookie who might one day lead the team to NFL glory. Would he really risk injury by trying to block a defensive player in a meaningless late-season game?

Yes.

That answer reflects why Wentz, once an unknown from North Dakota State, has a chance to be one of the NFL's best players for years to come.

"He's a beast, bro," Philadelphia receiver Jordan Matthews told ESPN's Tim McManus.[1]

It was the fourth quarter of a late December 2016 game against the New York Giants. The Eagles, with a chance to win after five straight losses, ran a running play with receiver Nelson Agholor. Wentz was ahead of him, looking for someone to block. Sprinting into view was New York defensive back Eli Apple, who was 6-1 and 194 pounds. The 6-5, 237-pound Wentz could have just tried to get in Apple's way. Instead, he hit Apple with his right shoulder—his throwing shoulder. Quarterbacks usually try to protect their throwing shoulders at all costs.

Eli Apple grew up in Philadelphia, but as a New York Giants defensive back, he wasn't about to take it easy on the Eagles or on quarterback Carson Wentz.

Wentz didn't think about that. He just wanted to win. He made the block even though he was already banged up. A few minutes earlier, he had been briefly knocked out of the game from a hit by Giants defensive end Olivier Vernon. Doctors kept him out for a few plays while they checked to see if he had a concussion. He came back, scrambled for an 11-yard run, and then made the block that helped the Eagles win, 24-19.

That kind of toughness impressed teammates.

"He's backyard football at its finest," Matthews told McManus after the game. "He's a great person to have as your quarterback. . . . That's what he wants to do. When you have a guy like that, then everybody wants to be around him."[2]

The Eagles hope to be around him for years to come.

"When you talk about Carson," Eagles executive vice president of football operations Howie Roseman said in Carson's team biography, "you're talking about a blue-collar quarterback. The guy has incredible work ethic. He's got incredible passion. He fits into the personality of this city, and you see that when he plays."[3]

Carson impresses because he cares. He doesn't get rattled when things go wrong, as they so often do, because he is strong of faith and discipline and duty. Those are among the reasons Philadelphia made a big trade with the Cleveland Browns to draft him in the spring of 2016.

Five months after the draft, Wentz began his NFL career with a bang. He was a superstar for the first three games, and a struggling newcomer for the next eleven. A bad offensive line left him a target for fiery defensive players wanting to hit him hard and often, and they did. Inconsistent receivers either didn't get open or dropped well-thrown passes.

Wentz didn't rattle. He took the blame because that's what leaders do. He kept learning. He escaped the rush when he could, threw the ball away when he had to. He made plays when it seemed hopeless. He found his third and fourth receiver options when most rookies would be stuck on one or two.

Teammates saw that he didn't give up on them—and they didn't give up on him. They believed in him and themselves.

Opponents were impressed.

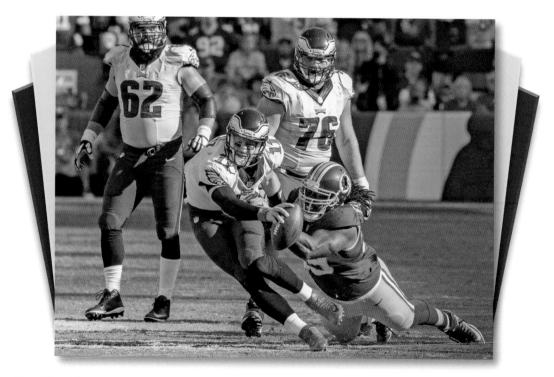

The Washington Redskins were among the teams to make it tough on Wentz as he dealt with the ups and downs of playing in the NFL.

Seattle cornerback Richard Sherman, known as much for speaking his mind as his NFL superstar play, liked what he saw from Wentz.

Seattle Seahawks Richard Sherman saw Wentz's potential after Seattle beat the Eagles 26-15 during the 2016 season. Wentz was 23-for-45 for 218 yards, two touchdowns (TDs) and two interceptions in that game.

"He was poised," Sherman said. "He wasn't shook. He's a rook. That's what he is."[4]

Did Wentz make mistakes? Sure. But Philadelphia offensive coordinator Frank Reich knew Wentz could handle it.

"Trust me, this guy is . . . mentally and physically very tough, and he's very mature," Reich told *Philadelphia Inquirer* columnist Bob Ford. "Because you've got to be to play the position and certainly to play here in this city, and he welcomes that, and we welcome that. We're glad we have him."[5]

Wentz proved Reich right by finishing strong, leading the Eagles to an upset of those playoff-bound Giants, then another over the Dallas Cowboys in the final two games of the 2016 season. Overall, Wentz threw for 3,782 yards, 16 touchdowns, and 14 interceptions. He set an NFL rookie record for most completions, with 379.

His passing yards were the fourth-most ever by a rookie, trailing Andrew Luck (4,374 in 2012), Cam Newton (4,051 in 2011) and Jameis Winston (4,042 in 2015). They were also the fourth-most in team history behind Donovan McNabb (3,916 in 2008 and 3,874 in 2004) and Randall Cunningham (3,808 in 1988).

Not bad for a guy who wasn't supposed to play until 2017.

"He's going to be a great player for a long time," Seattle quarterback Russell Wilson told *CSN Philly*. "He's athletic. He can make all the throws. [The Eagles] have a good one."[6]

Wentz was the second overall pick in the 2016 NFL draft, a big quarterback from a small school. People figured he needed time before he was NFL ready.

Philadelphia coach Doug Pederson said after the draft that the team wanted Wentz to learn the offense and all the NFL challenges without having to play right away. He insisted veteran Sam Bradford would be the starter, with Chase Daniel as backup.

As it turned out, Pederson was wrong.

Wentz, Philadelphia coach Doug Pederson (far right) and other Eagles officials celebrated Wentz's joining the organization.

A park eagle statue wasn't the only thing soaring in Bismarck, North Dakota, Carson's hometown.

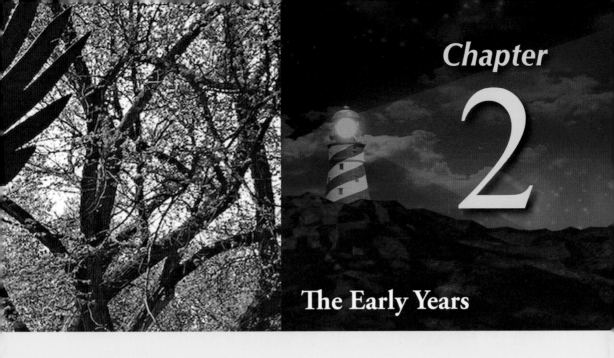

Carson Wentz was born on December 30, 1992, in Raleigh, North Carolina, to Cathy Domres and Doug Wentz. He has two brothers, Zach and Luke. When he was three years old, the family moved to North Dakota.

Sports were big in Carson's family. His father played linebacker at Northern State University in South Dakota. Brother Zach was a four-year starting pitcher and infielder at North Dakota State, good enough to set school career records for hits and doubles. A cousin, Connor, played tight end for North Dakota State from 2013 to 2015.

In fact, Carson's first job was umpiring youth baseball games.

Zach Wentz was a big motivator. Zach, who is three years older, was also a good student and a fierce competitor. The brothers had a lot of battles growing up.

"He has always been a role model," Carson said about his big brother in his Eagles bio. "I wanted to do better than him. I always wanted to follow in his footsteps."[1]

Carson grew up cheering for the Minnesota Vikings, but his favorite player was Green Bay Packers quarterback Brett Favre. "I loved watching Favre play," Carson said in his Eagles bio. "I loved his gunslinger mentality

Carson's mother, Cathy Domres, was proud of her son even before he became an NFL quarterback with the Eagles.

and the way he had fun. He was fun to watch, and he played the game the right way."[2]

Carson arrived at Bismarck Century High School so small, he might have been better off running cross country. He was 5-8 and 125 pounds as a freshman, and then started growing. As a sophomore, he was 5-10 and 150 pounds. As a junior, he was 6-3 and 170. By the time he was a senior, he was 6-5 and 200 pounds, plenty big enough to be a quarterback in high school and beyond.[3]

Still, many only saw him as Zach's younger brother. Sometimes newspaper photos referred to Carson as Zach. Game announcers even called him Zach.

That stopped when Carson's good play forced people to know his name.

One person who believed in him was Bismarck Century coach Nick Walker, who told him, "You have the ability to be great."[4]

"Just to hear that when you're smaller than everyone out there, it was pretty special," Wentz said in his bio. "He believed in me and expected to get the best out of me."[5]

Mission accomplished.

Carson played quarterback and defensive back in high school. In 2010, he was named North Dakota Class 3A Player of the Year, which is the division for the biggest schools in the state. He earned all-state honors.

As a senior quarterback, Carson threw for 1,285 yards and 12 touchdowns. He also ran for 553 yards and 13 TDs. As a defensive back, he totaled 61 tackles and two interceptions.

He also was a three-year starter for Bismarck Century's baseball team as a first baseman, hitting .386 with 26 runs batted in as a junior. In his senior year, Century was the state runner-up. Carson also played forward and center for Century's No. 1–ranked basketball team.

Beyond that, he was an excellent student. He made the National Honor Society with a 4.0 grade point average, and was the school's valedictorian. This honor is awarded to the student who has the highest grade point average in the senior class.

Still, only small colleges such as Southern Illinois, South Dakota State, North Dakota, and North Dakota State offered him football scholarships, and their interest had limits. Bismarck Century coach Ron Wingenbach called it "lukewarm."[6]

Recruiting picked up when a larger school, Central Michigan, recruited him late, but Carson had already made up his mind.

He was going to be a North Dakota State Bison.

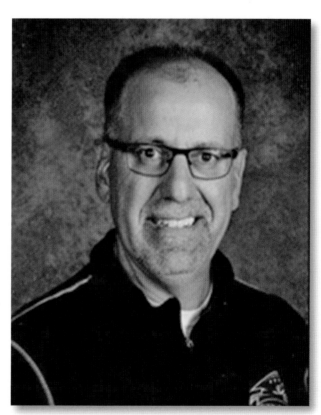

Bismarck Century High School football coach Ron Wingenbach made the most of Carson's talents by playing him on offense and defense.

It took Wentz three years to break into the starting lineup at North Dakota State. It paid off as he helped the Bison win national titles in his last two seasons.

College
Record Setter

North Dakota State played in the Football Championship Subdivision (FCS), which is for smaller schools. Big colleges such as Michigan, UCLA (University of California – Los Angeles), and Alabama play in the Football Bowl Subdivision (FBS). The main difference is the number of scholarships each team can give. FCS programs have only 65 scholarships. FBS schools are allowed 85.

Among FCS schools, North Dakota State was a superpower. It not only beat teams its own size, but far bigger ones. For instance, in 2016 the Bison upset No. 13 Iowa of the Big Ten Conference in Iowa City. In 2014, they beat Iowa State of the Big 12 Conference.

Wentz didn't play his first season at North Dakota State. Instead, he redshirted. This means he just practiced and worked out and took classes, but he didn't play. Even without him, the Bison won the 2011 national championship.

He was a reserve the next two seasons, which ended with North Dakota State winning national titles. Wentz played in 19 games, throwing for 353 yards and three touchdowns, and rushing for 92 yards and one TD.

As a junior he became the starter and led the Bison to a 15-1 record and another national championship. In his first college start, against much larger Iowa State, he completed 18 of 28 passes for 204 yards in a 34–14 upset win. During the FCS playoffs, he had three fourth-quarter comeback victories, and earned championship game Most Valuable Player honors.

Wentz set a school single-season record by throwing for 3,111 yards. He had 25 touchdown passes against 10 interceptions. He also was the team's second-leading rusher with 642 yards—the most by a Bison quarterback in 20 years—and six touchdowns.

He was ready for an even bigger senior season.

Before North Dakota State, no football team had won five straight national titles since the Wild West days, specifically when Yale unofficially won six straight championships from 1879 to 1884. Wentz was determined to lead the Bison to that fifth straight title. He had a strong first six games, but a broken wrist knocked him out of the next eight games. He didn't return until the FCS national title contest in January against Jacksonville State in Texas.

Wentz was more than ready. He completed 16 of 29 passes for 197 yards and a touchdown. He also ran for 79 yards and two TDs. North Dakota State dominated in a 37-10 victory, and Wentz was again named the game's Most Valuable Player.

"You can tell [Wentz] totally cares about this program," Bison receiver Zach Vraa said. "To see him come out in this game just showed the team and everybody else what we can overcome."[1]

In half a season Wentz threw for 1,651 yards, 17 touchdowns, and four interceptions while completing 63 percent of his passes. He also rushed for 294 yards and six TDs.

North Dakota State was 20-3 with Wentz as the starter, and 71-5 during his five years in the program. He finished third in school history in passing yards (5,115), touchdown passes (45), and career completion percentage (64.1 percent).

Wentz made a difference by running as well as throwing for his college team. He would continue to scramble to avoid getting sacked in the NFL.

Beyond that, he had a 4.0 grade point average as a senior while majoring in health and physical education. In 2014 and 2015, he made Academic All-American honors.

He was ready to move to the NFL. There was talk of a team drafting him in the first round. A lot of people wondered if he was good enough.

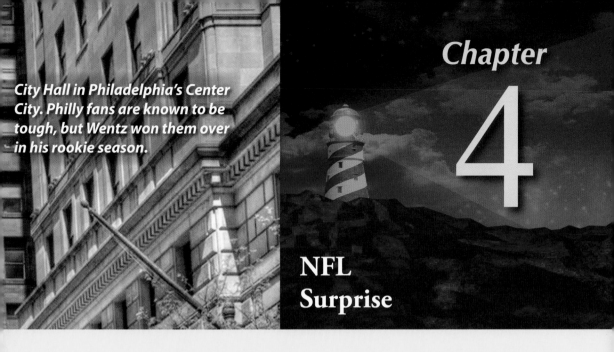

City Hall in Philadelphia's Center City. Philly fans are known to be tough, but Wentz won them over in his rookie season.

NFL Surprise

For those evaluating Wentz's NFL draft prospects, seeing wasn't always believing. Some scouts called him a risk, that he was "overrated" and not first-round material.[1] They found flaws in his fundamentals. That he had broken his right wrist (his throwing hand) as a college senior counted against him. And he had played against lightly regarded FCS competition. One scout called drafting such a small-school quarterback in the first round "scary business."[2]

Others saw Wentz as a diamond in the rough, a player who needed a couple of years of learning before becoming a quality starter. They liked his size (6-6, 237 pounds), arm strength, and toughness, plus the fact that he thrived in a pro-style passing attack at North Dakota State.

Wentz was impressive in the NFL Combine in Indianapolis. That is where most of the top draft hopefuls are tested physically and mentally by NFL coaches and scouts. Wentz finished among the top three quarterbacks in the 40-yard dash (4.77 seconds), the broad jump (9 feet, 10 inches), and the three-cone drill (6.86 seconds).

Some NFL draft experts predicted the Cleveland Browns would take Wentz with the NFL Draft's No. 2 pick. Former NFL coach Jon Gruden, a TV analyst, said in an ESPN feature, "I think he's the most NFL-ready quarterback that we've had in the last couple of years."[3]

Then there was the Wonderlic test, which is given to all NFL draft hopefuls. This intelligence test is designed to show how well a person can learn and solve problems.

Wentz got a score of 40 out of 50, which was considered excellent.[4]

This was more than enough to convince Philadelphia officials. Wanting to make sure no one else took him, they gave up three draft picks in the 2016 draft, their 2017 first-round choice, and a 2018 second-round pick to move up from No. 13 in the draft and get Cleveland's No. 2 pick.

Wentz became the highest FCS quarterback taken in the draft in history. The Eagles signed him to a four-year contract worth $26.7 million. He received a signing bonus of $17.6 million.

This did not make Philadelphia starting quarterback Sam Bradford happy. He asked the Eagles to trade him and stopped going to voluntary offseason

Wentz celebrated with NFL commissioner Roger Goodell after he became the No. 2 overall pick in the 2016 NFL draft.

workouts for a few days. As a veteran who had just signed a two-year, $35 million deal, Bradford wanted to play for a team that wanted him.

And so he did in 2016—for the Minnesota Vikings. Philadelphia traded him just before the season started.

A rib injury limited Wentz to just one preseason exhibition game, but he was ready for the season opener. He couldn't have started any better, leading the Eagles to a 3-0 record, including a win over Super Bowl contender Pittsburgh Steelers. He averaged 256 passing yards a game with five touchdowns and no interceptions.

Then came six losses in the next eight games. Wentz threw more interceptions than touchdowns, and rated 25th among the 32 starting quarterbacks.[5]

He didn't get down. He kept pushing the positive. After a loss to the Cincinnati Bengals during which he threw three interceptions, he tweeted, "Tough one today . . . But no time to be negative! Gotta stay positive and keep things in perspective. #AO1"[6]

Like most young quarterbacks, Wentz had to improve his form. His throwing motion wasn't as good as it needed to be, so he sometimes threw bad passes. Some evaluators said his windup was too long and needed to be shortened. Others said he sometimes threw at bad angles.[7] The key for an NFL quarterback is to get the ball out fast, on time, and accurately.

The Eagles had planned to work with Wentz on his fundamentals in 2016, but that changed when he became the starter. There wasn't time to do that.

Wentz was durable. He started all 16 games, the first Philadelphia quarterback to do that since Donovan McNabb in 2008. Only 13 other quarterbacks did that in 2016, and only one other rookie did it—Dallas's Dak Prescott. Only two other quarterbacks, New Orleans' Drew Brees and Tampa Bay's Jameis Winston, played more than Wentz. Not bad for a guy who missed a bunch of games in high school and college because of injuries.

"I'm very fortunate," Wentz told the *Philadelphia Inquirer*'s Zach Berman. "[A lot of it] goes to the guys up front doing a great job of protecting me."[8]

Wentz understood he is only as good as the teammates around him.

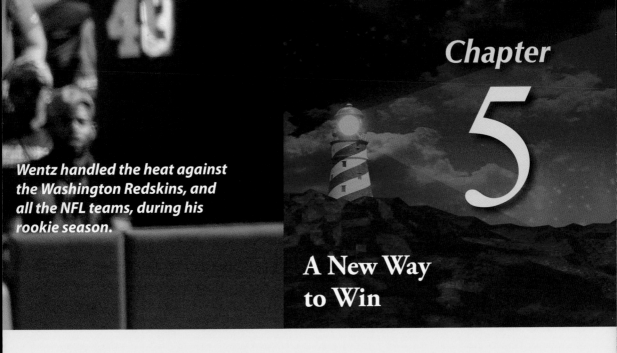

Wentz handled the heat against the Washington Redskins, and all the NFL teams, during his rookie season.

A New Way to Win

Wentz showed his tough game play again in December 2017. In the third quarter against the Los Angeles Rams, he made a first-and-goal scramble that landed him between two Rams players. He tore a ligament in his knee on the play, but got up and continued the series until the Eagles scored a touchdown. He would be out for the rest of what had been a stellar season. In 13 games he threw for 3,296 yards, 33 touchdowns, and seven interceptions. He completed 60.2 percent of his passes and had a quarterback rating of 101.9. Philadelphia was 11-2, and before the injury, Wentz was favored to win the NFL's most valuable player award.

Now that award was out of reach. But that would not stop Wentz from helping the Eagles prepare for the playoffs and the Super Bowl. He helped his backup, Nick Foles, lead the Eagles to the championship. They watched film together, and Wentz sent Foles encouraging notes and advice. As Wentz watched from the sidelines, Foles led the Eagles to a 41-33 Super Bowl victory over the New England Patriots.

The day after the Super Bowl, Wentz asked girlfriend Madison Oberg to marry him. She said yes.

Wentz has always made doing the right thing a priority. The tattoo on his right wrist—"AO1" (Audience of One) reflects that. It means, Live for God, and not for others. He has made it his life motto. During the 2016 season, he and his teammates wore cleats that had "AO1" on one shoe and the Bible verse location "Romans 5:8" on the other. It was part of an NFL social campaign called My Cause My Cleats to help raise money for charity. In 2017, he created the Carson Wentz AO1 Foundation to help those with physical, mental, and financial challenges.

Wentz said AO1 was "kind of a motto I picked up early in my career, and I finally put it on my body just to live [with] the Lord as my audience, whether it was playing football, going to school or whatever I'm doing in my life."[1]

The Romans verse reads: "God demonstrates His own love toward us, in that while we were still sinners, Christ died for us."

Faith is very much part of Wentz's life. So is respecting and appreciating fans. He does the extra things many won't, because he can and because he wants to.

For instance, near the end of his rookie season, a seven-year-old boy named Jude wrote him a letter. Jude said he was a big Eagles fan and that Wentz was his favorite player. He asked Wentz five questions. Wentz took the time to answer.

Question: What is your favorite color? Answer: Red
Question: Who is your favorite football player? Answer: Brett Favre
Question: Do you like Philly cheesesteaks? Answer: Of course I do!
Question: What is your favorite animal? Answer: Dogs!
Question: What is your favorite food? Answer: Steak

Then Wentz wrote, "Appreciate the support buddy! God bless!"[2]

Jude's grandmother was very grateful Wentz took the time. "Thank you again for your reply," she wrote. "You really did make Jude's day! I have never been prouder to be an Eagles fan."[3]

Wentz has always cared about helping others. That is why, if he weren't a quarterback, he'd probably be a high school teacher and coach.[4]

To get away from the pressures of the NFL, Carson likes to go hunting or to spend time with his dog, a golden retriever named Henley. He hopes to someday hunt in Alaska and travel around Europe.

In the end, next to his faith, playing football is what matters most. Wentz helped Philadelphia win a Super Bowl from the sidelines. Someday he hopes to win one on the field.

The Vince Lombardi trophy at the Philadelphia Art Museum. It reflects the impact Wentz has had on the Eagles, both on and off the field.

1992 Carson Wentz is born on December 30 in Raleigh, North Carolina.

1995 Carson and his family move to Bismarck, North Dakota.

2007 Carson enters Bismarck Century High School. He becomes a three-sport standout, playing football, basketball, and baseball.

2011 In June Carson graduates from Century as class valedictorian. In August he begins North Dakota State football training camp. He redshirts his first season. The Bison win the FCS (Football Championship Subdivision) national title under coach Craig Bohl.

2012 Wentz becomes the backup quarterback to Brock Jensen. On September 22, he plays in his first college game. He goes 8-for-8 in passing for 93 yards and a touchdown as North Dakota State beats Prairie View A&M 66-7. It is the most he will play in any game. He finishes the season passing 12-for-16 for 144 yards and two touchdowns. North Dakota State again wins the national championship.

2013 Wentz is again the backup quarterback behind Jensen. On October 13, in a win over Delaware State, he goes 10-for-13 for 105 yards and a touchdown. He finishes the season 22-for-30 for 209 yards and a touchdown. The Bison again win the national championship.

2014 Wentz becomes the starter. In the season opener, he goes 18-for-28 for 204 yards as North Dakota State beats the Big 12's Iowa State 34-14. On October 10, he catches a 16-yard touchdown pass from running back John Crockett on a trick play as North Dakota State rallies for a 17-10 win over Western Illinois. He later throws for 247 yards and five touchdowns in a win at Missouri State. He is named Academic All-American.

2015 On January 10, North Dakota State plays Illinois State in the national title game. Wentz throws for 287 yards and a touchdown in a 29-27 victory. His five-yard rushing TD with 37 seconds left is the game winner. The Bison finish 15-1 and win their fourth straight national title. On October 10, Wentz throws for a career-high 335 yards in a win over Northern Iowa. In the next game, against South Dakota, he breaks his right wrist in the first half. He still finishes the game, going 16-for-28 for 195 yards. The Bison lose. He misses the next eight games. He again is named Academic All-American.

2016 In January, Wentz plays in the national title game and wins game MVP honors. North Dakota State wins its fifth straight national championship. In late January Wentz plays in the Senior Bowl. He goes 6-for-10 for 50 yards. In February he participates in the NFL Combine in Indianapolis. He is in the top three among all quarterbacks in the 40-yard dash, broad jump, and three-cone drill. He also scores 40 out of 50 on the Wonderlic test. On April 28, Wentz is selected as the No. 2 overall pick by Philadelphia. He signs a four-year, $26.7 million contract. On September 11, Wentz plays in his first NFL game. He sets an NFL rookie season record by completing 379 passes. His 607 pass attempts are a team record and the second-most ever by a rookie in NFL history.

2017 In the offseason, Wentz has laser eye surgery so that he no longer needs to wear contact lenses. He creates the Carson Wentz AO1 Foundation. He throws for at least 304 yards in each of the season's first three games, with eight total touchdowns. He leads Philadelphia to an 11-2 start. He suffers a season-ending knee injury in a win over the Los Angeles Rams. On December 13, he has knee surgery. On December 19, he is named to his first Pro Bowl, but he cannot play.

2018 On February 4, the Eagles win the Super Bowl over the New England Patriots, 41-33. Wentz joins his teammates on their victory parade through Philadelphia. He and Madison Oberg get engaged.

STATISTICS

Passing

SEASON	TEAM	GP	CMP	ATT	CMP%	YDS	AVG	TD	LNG	INT	FUM	QBR	RAT
2016	PHI	16	379	607	62.4	3,782	6.23	16	73	14	9	55.4	79.3
2017	PHI	13	265	440	60.2	3,296	7.49	33	72	7	4	74.4	101.9
Career	PHI	29	644	1,047	61.5	7,078	6.76	49	73	21	13	--	88.7

Rushing

SEASON	TEAM	GP	ATT	YDS	AVG	LNG	TD	FD	FUM	LST
2016	PHI	16	46	150	3.3	17	2	15	4	1
2017	PHI	13	64	299	4.7	24	0	26	5	2
Career	PHI	29	110	449	4.1	24	2	41	9	3

CHAPTER NOTES

Chapter 1
1. McManus, Tim. "Carson Wentz Endearing Himself to Eagles, Philly with Blue-collar Play." ESPN.com. December 23, 2016.
2. Ibid.
3. Philadelphia Eagles. "Carson Wentz Bio."
4. Pelissero, Tom. "Richard Sherman on Carson Wentz? 'He Wasn't Shook. He's a Rook.' " *USAToday.* November 20, 2016.
5. Ford, Bob. "Eagles' Reich: Losing Finally Getting to Carson Wentz." *Philadelphia Inquirer.* December 6, 2016.
6. Sessler, Marc. "Russell Wilson on Carson Wentz: He's Going to Be Great." NFL.com. November 18, 2016.

Chapter 2
1. Philadelphia Eagles. "Carson Wentz Bio."
2. Ibid.
3. Kolpack, Jeff. "Bison QB Wentz Kept Growing in High School." *Bismarck Tribune.* October 31, 2014.
4. Philadelphia Eagles. "Carson Wentz Bio."
5. Ibid.
6. Kolpack.

Chapter 3
1. Peterson, Eric. "Bison Earn Place in College Football History with Fifth Straight FCS Title." Inforum.com. January 9, 2016.

Chapter 4
1. Goodbread, Chase. "Personnel Exec: There's No Way I Would Draft Wentz in Round 1." 24/7.com, February 5, 2016.
2. Goodbread, Chase. "Zierlein: North Dakota State QB Wentz Deserves First-Round Grade." 24/7.com, December 12, 2015.
3. Sheridan, Phil. "QB Carson Wentz, the No. 2 Overall Draft Pick, Agrees to Deal with Eagles." ESPN.com. May 13, 2016.
4. Conway, Tyler. "Carson Wentz, Jared Goff's Reported Scores on Wonderlic Test Revealed." *Bleacher Report.* March 28, 2016.
5. Kerr-Dineen, Luke. "Carson Wentz Has Been Quietly Terrible Since His Blazing Hot Start." *USAToday.* November 29, 2016.
6. Caron Wentz on Twitter: https://twitter.com/cj_wentz/status/805536408005906432
7. Robinson, Charles. "There's Something Wrong with Carson Wentz's Throwing Style and NFL Teams Are Catching On." *Yahoo Sports.* December 4, 2016.

8.   Berman, Zach. "Wentz Shows Eagles Durability by Starting Every Game This Season." *The Inquirer.* December 28, 2016.

Chapter 5
1.   Campitelli, Enrico. "Carson Wentz Is Wearing Bible Verse Cleats This Week." CSNphilly.com. November 30, 2016.
2.   Koller, Brock. "Eagles Quarterback Carson Wentz Answers 7-Year-Old Fan's Questions on Twitter." WPVI Philadelphia. December 13, 2016.
3.   Ibid.
4.   Philadelphia Eagles. "Carson Wentz Bio."

FURTHER READING

Works Consulted

Berman, Zach. "Wentz Shows Eagles Durability by Starting Every Game This Season." *The Inquirer.* December 28, 2016. http://www.philly.com/philly/sports/eagles/20161229_Wentz_shows_Eagles_durability_by_starting_every_game_this_season.html

Campitelli, Enrico. "Carson Wentz Is Wearing Bible Verse Cleats This Week." CSNphilly.com. November 30, 2016. http://www.csnphilly.com/the700level/carson-wentz-wearing-bible-verse-cleats-week

Conway, Tyler. "Carson Wentz, Jared Goff's Reported Scores on Wonderlic Test Revealed." *Bleacher Report.* March 28, 2016. http://bleacherreport.com/articles/2628221-carson-wentz-jared-goffs-reported-scores-on-wonderlic-test-revealed

Eckel, Mark. "Eagles' Worst Nightmare: What If Carson Wentz Isn't That Good?" NJ.com. December 6, 2016. http://www.nj.com/eagles/index.ssf/2016/12/eagles_worst_nightmare_what_if_carson_wentz_isnt_t.html

Fierro, Nick. "Carson Wentz Sets Rookie Completion Record as Eagles Finish Season." *The Morning Call.* January, 2017. http://www.mcall.com/sports/football/eagles/mc-eagles-notebook-0101-20170101-story.html

Ford, Bob. "Eagles' Reich: Losing Finally Getting to Carson Wentz." *Philadelphia Inquirer* December 6, 2016. http://www.philly.com/philly/sports/eagles/20161207_Eagles_OC_Reich__Losing_finally_getting_to_Carson_Wentz.html

Goodbread, Chase. "Personnel Exec: There's No Way I Would Draft Wentz in Round 1." 24/7.com. February 5, 2016. http://www.nfl.com/news/story/0ap3000000632864/article/personnel-exec-theres-no-way-i-would-draft-wentz-in-round-1

—. "Zierlein: North Dakota State QB Wentz Deserves First-Round Grade." 24/7.com, December 12, 2015. http://www.nfl.com

Kerr-Dineen, Luke. "Carson Wentz Has Been Quietly Terrible Since His Blazing Hot Start." *USAToday.* November 29, 2016. http://ftw.usatoday.com/2016/11/carson-wentz-philadelphia-eagles-gren-bay-packers-score-stats-hot-start-overrated

Koller, Brock. "Eagles Quarterback Carson Wentz Answers 7-Year-Old Fans' Questions on Twitter." WPVI Philadelphia. December 13, 2016. http://6abc.com/sports/eagles-qb-wentz-responds-to-7-year-old-fans-letter/1653187/

Kolpack, Jeff. "Bison QB Wentz Kept Growing in High School." *Bismarck Tribune.* October 31, 2014. http://bismarcktribune.com/sports/college/bison-qb-wentz-kept-growing-in-high-school/article_a9f0d1a8-6180-11e4-846e-63ce1bc183e9.html

McLane, Jeff. "McLane: Carson Wentz Looks Forward to Recharging After Taxing Year." Philly.com. January 13, 2017. http://www.philly.com/philly/sports/20170115_McLane__Carson_Wentz_looks_forward_to_recharging_after_taxing_year.html

McManus, Tim. "Carson Wentz Endearing Himself to Eagles, Philly with Blue-Collar Play." ESPN.com. December 23, 2016. http://www.espn.com/blog/philadelphia-eagles/post/_/id/19794/carson-wentz-endearing-himself-to-teammates-city-with-blue-collar-play

—. "Eagles Wear Carson Wentz's Life Motto, 'Audience of One,' on Their Cleats." ESPN.com. December, 2016. http://www.espn.com/blog/philadelphia-eagles/post/_/id/19434/eagles-wear-carson-wentzs-life-motto-audience-of-one-on-their-cleats

Patra, Kevin. "Carson Wentz Named Eagles' Starting Quarterback." NFL.com. September 5, 2016. http://www.nfl.com/news/story/0ap3000000695354/article/carson-wentz-named-eagles-starting-quarterback

Pelissero, Tom. "Richard Sherman on Carson Wentz? 'He Wasn't Shook. He's a Rook.'" USAToday. November 20, 2016. http://www.usatoday.com/story/sports/nfl/seahawks/2016/11/20/richard-sherman-carson-wentz-philadelphia-eagles-seattle/94188690/

Peterson, Eric. "Bison Earn Place in College Football History with Fifth Straight FCS Title." Inforum.com. January 9, 2016. http://www.inforum.com/sports/3920882-bison-earn-place-college-football-history-books-fifth-straight-fcs-title

Philadelphia Eagles. "Carson Wentz Bio." http://media.philadelphiaeagles.com/media/155846/wentz-carson.pdf

Robinson, Charles. "There's Something Wrong with Carson Wentz's Throwing Style and NFL Teams Are Catching On." Yahoo Sports. December 4, 2016. http://sports.yahoo.com/news/theres-something-wrong-with-carson-wentzs-throwing-style-and-much-of-nfl-has-caught-on-011427565.html

Sessler, Marc. "Russell Wilson on Carson Wentz: "He's Going to Be Great." NFL.com. November 18, 2016. http://www.nfl.com/news/story/0ap3000000741867/article/russell-wilson-on-carson-wentz-hes-going-to-be-great

Sheridan, Phil. "QB Carson Wentz, the No. 2 Overall Draft Pick, Agrees to Deal with Eagles." ESPN.com. May 13, 2016. http://www.espn.com/nfl/story/_/id/15519925/qb-carson-wentz-no-2-overall-draft-pick-agrees-deal-philadelphia-eagles

Shorr-Parks, Eliot. "After Midseason Slump, Eagles' Carson Wentz Once Again Looking Like a Franchise Quarterback." NJ.com. December 25, 2015. http://www.nj.com/eagles/index.ssf/2016/12/after_midseason_slump_eagles_carson_wentz_once_aga.html

—. "Eagles' Carson Wentz Has a Fractured Rib, Might Miss Rest of Season." New Jersey.com. August 2016. http://www.nj.com/eagles/index.ssf/2016/08/eagles_carson_wentz_has_a_fractured_rib_might_miss.html

Stites, Adam. "Mike Trout Gave All the Eagles New Shoes, So Carson Wentz Gave Him a Touchdown Ball." SB Nation.com. January 1, 2017. http://www.sbnation.com/2017/1/1/14140274/mike-trout-philadelphia-eagles-gift-football-carson-wentz-zach-ertz

On the Internet

ESPN: Carson Wentz Stats
http://www.espn.com/nfl/player/_/id/2573079/carson-wentz

NFL.com: Carson Wentz
http://www.nfl.com/player/carsonwentz/2555259/profile

Philadelphia Eagles: Carson Wentz
http://www.philadelphiaeagles.com/team/roster/Carson-Wentz/cca3a1f1-e1c3-4282-8218-62b3d7b1d4f3

Big Ten—One of the major conferences in college sports. Originally made up of 10 universities, it now has 14, including Maryland, Ohio State, Michigan, Indiana, Iowa, Illinois, and Nebraska.

Big 12—One of the major conferences in college sports. Originally made up of 12 universities, it now has 10, including Kansas, Texas, Oklahoma, Oklahoma State, and West Virginia.

championship (CHAM-pee-un-ship)—A game that determines the best team in a given sport.

completion (kum-PLEE-shun)—A pass that is caught.

concussion (kun-KUH-shun)—An injury to the brain caused by a blow to the head.

conference (KON-frentz)—A group of teams that play one another during the regular season.

defensive (dee-FEN-siv) **back**—A defensive player whose main job is to make sure the other team does not catch a pass. He also has to tackle players who come his way. He plays in the back of the defense, the farthest away from the offense.

defensive (dee-FEN-siv) **end**—A big player who plays up front near the offensive line. He starts at the end of the line. His job is to tackle running backs and pressure the quarterback.

discipline (DIH-sih-plin)—The ability to act in a way that shows good judgment, or to do the right thing, no matter how hard.

durable (DUR-uh-bul)—Able to last and not wear down.

evaluator (ee-VAL-yoo-ay-tor)—Someone who judges or grades the performance of another.

FBS—Football Bowl Subdivision. A group of the biggest 120 or so college football programs in the country. Each one is allowed to give 85 scholarships.

FCS—Football Championship Subdivision. The college football programs that compete at the NCAA Division I level and are not in the FBS.

fundamentals (fun-dah-MEN-tuls)—The basic physical skills in a given sport, such as good footwork in football.

gunslinger mentality (GUN-sling-er men-TAL-ih-tee)—A term used for a quarterback who isn't afraid to throw passes all over the field, even if receivers aren't completely open.

inconsistent (in-kun-SIS-tent)—A performance that is up and down, sometimes good, sometimes not.

interception (in-ter-SEP-shun)—A pass that is caught by an opposing defensive player.

ligament (LIH-guh-ment)—A tough band of tissue that connects bones and helps control motion.

NFL—National Football League. The organization that runs and regulates professional football.

NFL Combine (KOM-byn)—A week-long period each year during which NFL coaches and scouts test college prospects before the NFL Draft.

NFL Draft—A multiday period in April when NFL teams select the best college players for their teams.

offensive coordinator (aw-FEN-siv koh-OR-dih-nay-tor)—In football, the coach who is in charge of running the offense. He comes up with the style of offense, and the plays. He calls the plays during a game.

playoffs—A series of games for which only the top teams qualify and that determines which one is the best.

potential (poh-TEN-shul)—Something that a person or team is capable of doing, but hasn't yet done.

quarterback (KWOR-ter-bak)—In football, the player who runs the offense. He calls the plays, throws passes, hands the ball to teammates, and sometimes runs. He is like the coach on the field.

rookie (RUH-kee)—An athlete in his or her first year of professional competition.

running back—In football, a player whose main job is to gain yards by running. On pass plays, he has to block and protect the quarterback, or go out and catch a pass.

scramble (SKRAM-bul)—In football, when a quarterback has to run for yards when his blocking breaks down and defensive players are about to tackle him for a loss of yards.

touchdown (TUTCH-down)—In football, when a team moves the ball into the end zone. It is worth six points.

trade—To give one thing for another. In sports, one team will give another team a player in exchange for another player or players, or for money.

tweet—A short sentence or phrase used on the Internet through social media's Twitter program; to send such a message.

valedictorian (val-ih-dik-TOR-ee-un)—The high school or college senior who has the highest grade point average, and who gives the senior speech during graduation ceremonies.

Wonderlic (WUN-der-lik) **test**—An intelligence test designed to see how well a person can learn and solve problems.

PHOTO CREDITS: Cover, pp. 1, 4, 7, 14, 17, 22—Keith Allison; back cover—DPK Photography; p. 6—Disney/ABC; p. 8—Mark Samia; p. 9—FeedMeSports; p. 13—Blue Hawk Boosters; p. 18—Susan Procario; p. 20—Gaming Guy; p. 25—Governor Tom Wolf. All other photos—Public Domain. Every measure has been taken to find all copyright holders of material used in this book. In the event any mistakes or omissions have happened within, attempts to correct them will be made in future editions of the book.

INDEX